AF409284

Also by Bernard Jan

Novels

Cruel Summer

January River

Novella

Look for Me Under the Rainbow

Memoir

A World Without Color

POSTCARDS

FROM BEYOND

REALITY

The Selected Poems
of Michael Daniels

BERNARD JAN

Postcards From Beyond Reality: The Selected Poems of Michael Daniels

by

Bernard Jan

Published by Bernard Jan, Zagreb, 2022

Originally and first published in Croatian as *Razglednice s one strane stvarnosti – Odabrane pjesme Michaela Danielsa* by Hrvatska akademija znanosti i umjetnosti, Forum, mjesečnik razreda za književnost Hrvatske akademije znanosti i umjetnosti, Godište XXXXII. Knjiga LXXIV. Broj 1-3, Zagreb, spring 2003

Copyright © Bernard Jan 2022

All Rights Reserved.

No part of this book may be reproduced, stored, or transmitted in any form or by any means, electronic, mechanical, photocopying, recording, scanning, or otherwise, without permission in writing from the copyright owner, that is the author of this book. The only exception is by a reviewer, who may quote short excerpts in a review. No AI training: Any use or reproduction of any part of this publication for training artificial intelligence (AI) technologies or systems is expressly prohibited.

This is a work of fiction.

All characters in this work are fictitious. Any resemblance to actual persons, living or dead, is purely coincidental.

Editing by Claudette Cruz, The Editing Sweetheart

Proofreading by the Hyper-Speller at wordrefiner.com

Cover design by Jessica Bell

Print On-Demand: amazon.com

ISBN (Print On-Demand) 978-953-59581-8-5

Cataloguing-in-Publication data available in the Online Catalogue of the National and University Library in Zagreb under CIP record 001130252.

fROM bEYOND rEALITY

For Michael

A scream ruptured the darkness of a sleeping creature.

I have become aware of my existence!

hEART

What is the color of my heart while I hold it
in my hand and look amazed at the sun? And
what is the color of blood running down my palm
and disappearing in its pores? Leaving a trail.
And the seal of a time. Gentle, voiceless, and
evanescent like a breath; invisible from the light
that is burning my pupils.

A drop drops, and on a sleeve of my
(already dirty) shirt dances with the fire of the
distant torches and the smell of the scorched land.
Heart sighed. Almost silently. Afraid to disturb an idyll
of a day it has witnessed. And the moment.

And cognition.

(It came too late.)

Speechless, I watched it contort in the
determined clench of a fist, only now realizing
how nice it was to—live.

fAITH

The man believes in what he wants to believe.

I want to believe that Love exists.

sUMMER sYMPHONY

I am screaming to the boiling point!

Voice rough like sandpaper.

Asphalt sings a symphony under

the dancing wheels.

And I'm sweating . . .

It's summer.

tHE gREATEST sIN

"What is the greatest sin?"

"Not to repent . . . ?"

IIFE

I searched for it in the vastness of the universe and the

depth of the

darkness it breathed. In the whisper of the night and the

serenity of

the wilderness that surrounded me. In the milky shine of

the stars and

the silence of the moon while it disappeared behind a

cloud.

    Silently.

    Obediently.

    The grass has stopped growing—and for a

moment the

world seemed as though it ceased to exist. The flutter of

wings

carried by the wind through the night was unearthly real.

And then

the moon appeared again, and the stars dawned in full

splendor.

With benevolent dance of the locks on my forehead the wind
played with, I looked up, way up, and smiled. I didn't look for
anything anymore.

For I knew that life was in me!

uNFINISHED pOEM

When I open my eyes,

mornings tend to be soft and sickly gentle,

offering absolution on a gold platter of

oblivion, hope, and New York's madness.

When I open my eyes, a day seems cuddly

despite frustrated haste

of unsmiling faces. The colors are unspeakably clear

while I slide through the streets on the board.

(The envy-green of Central Park; the gray-blue

of the high, opaque-sky-like, tired eyes

of a young addict, jealousy-purple of the bruises

on my body; vibrating lecherous-red glow

of the nightclubs, blood, and sin; platinum bodies of the

surfers

on the Coney Island beaches; electric-blue

of the rebellious sky pierced by lightning.)

I enjoy and absorb every movement,

each reflection from the window glass while

the night slowly descends. The morning gives way

to the evening, joy hides from despair.

It's dreaming time . . .

Darkness covers the city losing the battle with

the lights of the city. But it wins my

soul chained with anxiety. Fear.

And predictability of forthcoming . . .

Dream . . . Time to dream.

The only beauty of New York I feel at night

when I can ride. Far. Long. Free.

Without thinking. Relaxed. Wild. Suicidal . . .

I appreciate that. I respect that. I LOVE that.

I reject the dream that will bring no rest or break

before the new ride. (I know that.) I refuse to dream

because I remember the earlier dreams. I remember

them too well . . .

I don't rest tired limbs tightened with hard,

healthy, and inflamed muscles; I stay up at night and

like a watchman near the end of the shift I count

minutes.

I remember, I count, and turn into one of . . .

dream collectors . . .

And I remember . . .

kNIFE

Warm was the drop of

light

which slid down the shining

knife blade. Less than

a moment ago

it shone

in somebody's eye!

iN sEARCH OF THE sUN
(In memory of watching Total Eclipse)

I'm cold.

I'm shaking and shivering in the warmth of the
street lamps.

I walk through the park; distracted and slow.
Almost strolling.
I think of the sun, which flew to the warmer places and
Rimbaud
while he searched for it. I feel that I understand him.
(At least I think so.)

The icy fingers of coming winter are
treacherously pinching my
unprotected body. Waking in me the longing for warmer
times. Will I have to go to Africa too? In search of
the sun that hid there?

The couple sat on the bench I walked past;
backpacks at

their feet. The sound of a kiss destroys with a flame a mind picture

of warm Africa. No ashes remained. But a breath of warmth that

it brought with it, somehow managed to get hold of me and

accompany me into the night.

I was no longer cold.

cLOUDS

I watch the clouds as they travel and imagine where the
next one will take me . . .

hOPE

In the basement of the soul strange flowers grew. With no light

and water they opened their petals in the dark. And released scents.

Diverse and not always pleasant. Sometimes so weak that they could be

hardly distinguished from the stench of the rot that surrounded them.

One scent was stronger than the others. More intense, persistent, and

pervasive. It made its way to the nostrils of the subconscious. Only

it needed one breath to full consciousness, one breath that never happened.

Thanks to it, there is still hope.

tHE sTEALER OF dREAMS

I hate you!
I HATE YOU!!!

Steal my dream one more time
and I will crush you. (This is not a threat!)

Dimensions of existing worlds
will collapse your refuge;
sweat spilled by force
will stop being sweet.

(The milk will get sour and the honey will become too
bitter.)

Because,

Sin has sown the field
and bore the fruit of shame,

nurturing the sprout with drops of silence.

While

in the ticking of the last hour
patience has not withered; the reaper is early.
The hand took away the dreams.

I don't hate you,
I don't hate you anymore . . .

Steal my dream one more time,
steal it if you can and keep me from dreaming.

The nights came down calm and breathed
air into my lungs. Choking them
with its flickering intoxicating sweetness.
Before the sleep overwhelmed me.

(No, I do not hate you anymore, Stealer . . .)

fANATIC

Exclusiveness!

Again . . . Why??

Which is the way to the balance?

The legs are already tired.

mIRAGE

I followed in the footsteps of the lost in the desert.

The sand of Sahara—impossibly hot, drains

the last drop out of me. Traces didn't stop.

I lift my head. I stretch my neck. My tongue

hanging out like in a fallen marathoner.

Kneeling in front of the waters that were calling me

from the foot of the dunes. So close, so damn

reachable. Hm, I knew I wouldn't be able to

make the slightest movement, but I wasn't

too concerned about that. No. Peace reigned

in me. Strange and alien. But still peace.

bOREDOM

I'll release the roar—

and be the wolf who growls at the moon full of despair;

envious and jealous of the beauty of its shine.

I will travel the seas and worlds—

a loner seeking change or oblivion—

and capsize the ships which in my anger I will

find.

I'll laugh with the whine of the wind at the screams

that cry for help and enjoy a little liveliness I

brought into the day. (Otherwise, I'm not prone to

killing,

but what else will I have left!)

Who will save the day?

I'll bring some chaos into the traffic

(as if this is not part of our everyday life);

but why don't we all have a little more

fun?

People, you can go crazy, for all I care,

just mute those damn sirens! They will

pierce my eardrums. And be careful not to kill

each other.

For, who else would save my day

and resurrect thoughts wrecked with boredom?

Who will tell me what to do with myself?

yOU'RE nOT hERE

I'm going through my crises,

and you're not here

to comfort me in your look

and invigorate the tired womb.

Hear the voice of the miserable man

who cries after you; he's calling you!

Spread the sails lowered

and sail, my sweet one, into the dead harbor.

There . . . I'm waiting for you.

tHE cURSE OF hERITAGE

I'm here today. I still am and exist.

I breathe, move, and live.

Someone I knew died this morning.

We weren't too close, but his departure

still crushed me. I struggle not to admit it

Not easy for me.

A glance out the window reveals to me

the rain falling. And the wet streets. How far pastures

are on which he now sleeps? Will I have the strength

to look for them? Will I have the courage?

To accept the challenge and face the curse

of heritage that has taken its toll.

sPRING

We kill each other

slowly,

driving ourselves crazy

and stealing precious hours.

Tenderness and words of love

we banished by the whip of

our tongues.

Insults! Malice! Wickedness!

Insurmountable humiliation.

What happened to remorse!?

Why snow covered the grass

and mowed the flowers of pansies?

Cold has frozen the breath of spring,

gloatingly grinning at the lovers.

wHEN i dIE

I defy you, winds!

Color the sky with voluptuous sounds of trumpets

the day I die and become one of you!

Pave heaven with laughter and tears

so the morning that dawns, dawns with clarity and joy

Of precious memories that I've left behind to walk into

A new day.

pROVIDENCE

I was early.

You were late.

To blame someone

that providence didn't favor us?

bELIEVE.

Believe it or not

I am the only one left

In these mournful dawns

Heart inspired with compassion

Faith and

Regret

The voice of the child has died

With the first light of

The morning sun

aBOUT rEDEMPTION

To cast a spell on you I want,

So I'm not the only one

Who remains last, but once was the first,

Known to everyone and then forgotten!

In the power of redemption of souls of ours

Do you believe now, my friend?

Or the morning that will dawn with good

Won't be good for us at all

dEATH cAN dANCE

My mind is collapsing under the

weight of the night.

The burden is heavy and tiresome.

Rest won't come.

Sparkles of illusions and

a world of troubled thoughts.

Blizzards of snow-born sorrows.

Flight of the sparrows

in frenzied flocks.

Coming and going away.

Into the night.

Into surrender.

Into oblivion.

Into the dark fogs of eternity.

I saw Death on my window.

It was gray.

And it was dancing . . .

iT iS A dREAM, iT iS dEATH, OR iT iS bOTH OF iT

In the end, I will die anyway.

So why keep worries that embitter our lives

and deepen our pain,

yelling and screams erupted with the passion

of drugged emotions?

What is the point, when the only thing I wish

is to reach the bottom and—vanish?

(I have no pride anymore.)

The heights are too distant and I don't crave for them.

(I only seek peace.)

And liberation of the morning—

in the night too distant, unreachable like a dream.

So I seek, but I cannot find.

(What?)

It is a dream, it is death,

or maybe it is both of it.

aWAKENINGS

I know I am good for nothing anymore:

17 awakenings (toward the end ever

longer and weary)—wasted time.

I don't regret for what *never*

happened, I don't mourn what

I *didn't* have.

With the fate of a fallen angel I stand

in the sunset and look at the summer,

in the waters of Bethesda rinsing the salt

of my tears.

Somehow I know I will not breathe

the smell of Central Park asphalt again.

tHE fIRST pART OF THE sTUMBLED tRILOGY

in

the

existential

luxury

of

endless

rows

of

shelves

shaken

and

stumbling

i

reach

for

the

only

remaining

bottle

of

coca-cola.

i'm full thirsty.

mEDITATION . . . bEFORE THE rAIN

Like a long-distance mass

The downpour was tiresome

And destroyed the perception

Of eager anticipation

It is best to withdraw into yourself

And suppress the passions

Of accumulated adrenaline

Until the anger is gone

And the culprit for abstinence

Gives an account

The purpose of existence then will be

Justified

aLIENATION

In collusion with: reality

I took: a teaspoon of illusions

and dissolved it in solution: of my own dreams.

Through a blurry game: of molecules

I watched: an abstract picture

of my mental state,

wondering:

WHAT AM I DOING HERE?!

a vIEW iNTO THE fUTURE

lIBERATION

I realized that I was subject to transience.

Nothing is forever, and neither are we.

The dawn of Armageddon is smiling at us—

To someone sinister, to someone

bringing liberation.

I would like to last a little longer . . .

(Than you.)

a cACOPHONY OF wORDS

A

landscape

torn

by

beauty

retreats

before

the

invasion

of

my

sk8board!

aN uNCONVENTIONAL pOEM

I am against all conventions.

Tyrants need to be destroyed,

but also a butterfly must be saved:

that gentle reflection of a child's innocence

lost in the daybreak of the New York night.

The penetration of light into the darkness of carnal

madness will prevent crime and

defeat the condemnation of the innocent.

That is the only way we can survive.

By the flashes of light, the flashes of

reason, the flashes of humanity.

UNCONVENTIONALLY.

mETAMORPHOSIS

I plunge into myself and rise

from the hell of personal experiences.

Michael will stop being Michael,

turned into an executioner of other people's weaknesses

and his own failures.

Crap needs to be dealt with once and for all!

Why not right now?? The monster is settled

and rests contentedly in its chambers

sprinkled with a mire of freshest

sin. Not anticipating the arrival of the angel of

vengeance,

not hearing the solid sound of liberating trumpets.

Tears poured out their anger; more than

ready, waiting for revenge.

Restrained by extreme effort, and once

an ancient but now outdated threat.

Michael stopped being Michael.

wAR aGAINST vIRUSES

I'm sick of powerlessness and stumbling; and I burn in a
fever of my own failures.
I urgently need a new dose of confidence.
It's not easy being a righteous person attacked by a virus
of amorality.

I've been thinking about changing the climate for a long
time.
(Not global, of course, but my personal, private one.)
Or perhaps, simply, shall I replace the antivirus program?
Upgrade to a newer, better, more resistant and stronger
version?

Whatever.
As long as it works, and I will be walking with my head
up again.

dEPARTURE

Wait for me, Mother,

and do not leave me in the tunnel of shadows.

Stop, Mother,

as I write this one last verse,

because for me there is nothing else here.

a pOSTCARD

If I send you a postcard

will you thank me for it?

Will you remember to call me,

prompted by curiosity to investigate

the appropriateness of a white background

of unwritten messages?

Your name—my name—and nothing more.

Like everything else.

Emptiness.

And the weary ships on its face

drifting away with full sails

each to its own world.

A grim reminder of our reality.

fORGIVENESS

In the fissure of anxiety

the man looks up to The Real One

expecting forgiveness to slide down

the airy thread of the evening light

skillfully like a spider,

and stop the tide of the lake overflowing

the dam and, spilling out, escaped from

the eyes red with remorse.

(17 iMAGES) fROM bEYOND rEALITY

A plastic sea, heaving with purple tulips;

Coral reefs overgrown with skyscrapers;

Asleep sun behind the red sky that guards over the
charred forests;

Phoenix pierced with a crossbow plunges over New
Queens;

Clouds swallowed by the flames of morbid torches of the
extinct KKK;

Dreams turned into reality;

Faces of New Yorkers painted with smiles;

The streets of New York—free skateboarding zone;

Resurrection of Titanic with fanfares and fireworks;

I walk on the Red Planet (fresh footprints in the sea of
silence);

The meeting with my father;

Return of innocence;

Mornings smelling of buds of late changes;

Daybreak of tolerance and victory of equality;

Locked fears and the pogrom of nightmares;

Rainbow in my eyes;

Peace among men.

tHE sECOND pART OF THE sTUMBLED tRILOGY

the

crests

of

waves

snatch

the

surfboard

from

under

my

feet

and

salt

my

throat

with

the

scorcher.

i

can

only

trust my instinct.

i sTAY

My sad city,

I give up all attempts

to fathom you with understanding

of a delighted child.

By distances pumped adrenaline

throbs in my temples with a silent call

and yet, somehow, I'm not moving . . .

I stand motionless in place, and I stay.

Bewitched by the nostalgia for your concrete.

tHE lAST OF THE vAMPIRES

It is more than I can endure,

It is even more than you can live with,

Yet who on Earth is to know

about the silent cry of immortality?

Nights are dead except for us and

colors are blind for everyone but me and you.

But when blood is dripping down our chin,

It is something that others can hear too.

iN rEUNION

Where darkness meets the horizon of my dawning
And angels spread their wings in heaven's glory

I come to you . . . from across the world
To lousily play a trumpet—even only for a short, phony
moment
You reach for me . . . to touch my soul
Melting bitterness of rainy days to come

Where black is blue, and milk is wine
Where mountains bloom with corns in yellow

You hear the song of a childhood smiling
Its giggling sound through the doors of the past
Prophesying

Visions of the days long gone by now
And sun still shining upon our heads

Cleaning tears and dirt from our salty faces

Where graves sing in silence
And surfers tend the first morning waves
Where everything old is new
And yet looks the same

You come to me
I reach for you
Again in reunion

tHE uMBRIAN sEA

All the springs will dry up sometime
and oil will stop soaking the land

The celestial torchbearers will extinguish
and eternal darkness prevails

When in the sharp glow of my gaze
Your breath freezes and disappears toward

the Umbrian Sea

tHE bLOODY rIVER

Darkness covered the heart with

the wings of doubt

And tackled us with

superfluous thinking

    Bruises

    Hematomas

    Paranoia-broken

    plates

    Distraught glances . . .

I bite your neck with the force of

untamable butcher

Rinsing INFIDELITY in the warmth of your blood

bitterness of my tears

and the still flow of the river

tHE eAST rIVER hAS bEGUN TO wEEP

The East River has begun to weep
Spilling its sorrow over the shallows
Of New Manhattan

Swaying algae on the anchors of sleeping giants
And gnawing at rusty steel of their hulls
Looking for me

Knowing I won't be here soon

A little longer . . .
And my body will disappear from these banks
Awoken with mornings with no future
And lulled to sleep with restless nights

A little longer and I am leaving without a trace

A pair of worn-out Droors pants

Is left in SoHo

And discarded memories

No one took notice of

sELF-pORTRAIT

Canons of light

with their reflection wash the

streets   squares   pools

parks—everything with asphalt

mirroring the sun

and its spots

on everything that moves,

everything that rolls

and ingratiatingly crawls

in the evening gust

of refreshing breeze that

crawls

from Long Island

and then rises along

the bridges of New Manhattan

and leaps over the running waters

and hums in the canopies

of blooming trees

intoxicating the soul of every

enthralled passerby.

The world is here and the world is mine

welcomed with arms wide open

accepted   captured   trapped

in the whirlwind of laughter

of playful skateboards.

I'm happy today! This is my paradise!

A moment to remember

No matter what will be tomorrow.

tHE lAST pART OF THE sTUMBLED tRILOGY

listening

to

the

retarding

beats

of

a

frightened

heart

i

gaze

at

the

only

remaining

drop

of

life

trying

to

turn

it

into

something

fantastic!

mASTODON

I spread my wings
Unrestrained like giant sequoias
and I sigh at the beauty of just leafed-out cedars

Doesn't anyone else feel
The warmth of life spilling out
from the newly awakened springs
There, in the depths of darkness
where no one needs to pretend what
they are
But remains forever and never ceases
to be

Doesn't anyone notice
how nice it is to be young
Although briefly and only temporarily
Free like an eagle
who captured by someone's photograph

never stops his flight

but stays

There, in the light of day

Where everyone thinks they see what

we are

But not caring for the reality hidden

behind the masks we wear

Overcome by a wild urge

to change EVERYTHING

I spread my wings and take off

knowing that someone would also capture my flight

I don't want to turn into a mastodon

a cYNIC

A cynic in me woke up

and danced in the summer shower of heavy words

The wretch in me spoke

with sour smiles of painful bites

by a dagger of tongue ripping someone else's intimacy

Blood was pouring from the injured eyes

As I fled into the bowels of the subway

A hidden world full of moisture, darkness, all kinds of

beings

and stench of the banished and lost like

me

I will be protected there and find my home

A little peace in the mother's womb

I will be there my own, cared for and loved

Before the morning vomits me into a new day

Once again disguising me as a cynic

hAIKU

Dude A

(pondering over a piece of paper)

Looks like haiku.

Dude B

(watching a skateboarder concentrating on a trick)

It isn't haiku.

Dude A

(not taking his eyes from the piece of paper in his hands)

It looks to me like haiku.

Dude B

(his full attention with the skater half-flipping into a darkslide *to*

fakie*)*

Told you. It ain't haiku.

Dude A

(looking at Dude B)

And what is it, then?

Dude B

(gasping with admiration at the skater turning his skateboard in their direction)

Just missed perfection.

Dude A

(not getting it)

Come again?

Dude B

(almost whispering)

Poetry in motion.

Victor—the skater who did the technically immaculate trick

(to Alien: Dude A and me: Dude B, wiping sweat from his shiny forehead)

What are you guys theorizing about?

Alien and **I**

(not looking at each other, with one voice)

Poetry!

iNDEPENDENT

Once I believed in You
and my life wasn't a farce
Once while I slept soothed
on the feeding breasts of my mother

Now, now I don't know anymore what it means
to be calm, and I don't try to understand
lofty goals they taught me
I should respect

So I am taking a running start and escaping from
everything
Hasting away from the eyes and alien looks
Eager to be different
Eager to be my own
Like a tattoo of the cross I carry on my leg
eager to be independent

cOLD iS THE wORLD

Cold is the world we are living in
and mornings do not warm us

Dawns are stale . . .

and they do not break with elation
of a child delighted with an ice cream

On the informational highway
of headless, destructive speeds
we keep up with the time
which irrevocably retreats into a frustrated past
with every outburst of anger

Leaving us alone,

headless, confused, tired,
drained, distraught, and

hungry for true love

Cold is the world we are living in
and there is no one to keep us warm
while the nights haunt us darker
than has ever been the case before

bIRDHOUSE

Now—when it's too late to change anything
turn back time and I retrace the footsteps that classified
me as one of heartless and insensitive people
I can eat myself alive with anguish, misery, resentment,
and guilt
for not picking up a dying pigeon with broken wings
from the road
because I looked away from the endless pleading of an
eye filled with painful agony
and I didn't give water to the beak which without a
sound cried out for drops of water I was carrying in my
backpack
in the spring heat
in the sea of passersby
car noise
with too little compassion

What would you do, Father, if I brought home a pigeon

with broken wings

Would you step on him and with one swing crush what

little life was still smoldering in him

enjoying the crisp sound of crushing remaining healthy

bones

Or maybe I'm wrong

And you would build a birdhouse for him so he could

always come back to you once healed

wake you up cooing and remain a faithful reminder of

your goodness while having the strength to perform

another looping—in your honor

Build him a home just like you did it for me and lock

him behind the net of secrets and sleepless fears

Every day, in the late afternoon, strollers would admire

this beautiful birdhouse again

not knowing how much trauma was left lying hidden

under the feathers behind the white-painted walls

zOO yORK

Day **One**

and a light appears on the horizon

and ships emerge from the light

Day **Two**

and the old civilization meets the new

and Man-a-hatt-ta becomes Manhattan

Day **Three**

and marshes, and hilly land, and vegetation, and local

animals are covered with concrete

and so begins day 4

Day **Four**

and skyscrapers connect heaven and earth

Day **Five**

and harbors open their gates in the face of another

invasion

and Manhattan gets the New prefix to its name

and part of New York turns into Zoo York

Day **Six**

and sometime at the end of day 6 I was born

Day **Seven**

and I sanctified day 7 to rest and skateboarding with my

friends

contrary to the working rhythm that continually splashes

this unusual island

tHE wORLD OF mENACE

Try as you might

But you won't be able to escape from who you

really are

(Some people call it faith

some people call it alter ego

some people call it curse

and I call it damnation)

You can run fast

You can skate even faster

and chase the wind with mighty power

of your hurting muscles

Yet, shadows are still with you

Always on the run and somewhere around

present and indestructible

This is another world

The world of Menace

With new rules to obey

And other forces to serve them

No one can take that away from you

Nothing you can do about it

Accept the reality and skate even faster

FOREVER

a pOEM FOR vICTOR

Everything comes to an end once

and the day goes down behind the glass walls of the

skyscrapers

drowning new promises in the silence of darkness

and the lurking dangers of branched canopy of

Central Park

We all end once

and a black cloud like the sulfur which scorches

Sodom and Gomorrah towers over us

devouring the vision of the future by the presentiment

of a miraculously awakened third eye

It sucks when you're young—

and imbued with a sense of transience and the image

of the metal sky that colored the world

I don't know if it was a closeness

or the telepathy of our friendship

But today I had you in vision again

and I wasn't too happy about it

The black cloud stole you once again

. . . i'M dYING INTO eTERNAL lIFE . . .

I'm dying last in a row

In a world where no one is left

and nothing but—OBJECTS,

Over which the dream descends

and erases the dusty remains of

wrath, love, and forgiveness.

The waters calm down and stop

to flow

turning them into ice

crystals

harvested from future civilizations.

It's my turn,

the last in a row and the sole

survivor,

to take off my hooded sweater,

roll up the sleeves (of my favorite shirt)

and start digging my grave.

In a cracked, withered earth,

in live and hot asphalt,

instead of a tombstone I stick

a board of a disassembled skateboard.

The time has come:

I'm dying as a skater

and I'm dying as a man,

and I grow into a tradition of Poe.

With inspiration, I clone his

shadow

and curled up under the wing of a new experience;

I start living forever . . .

tHE eND OF mE

This is the end of me.
The end of time,
One life I no longer wish to
soak up.

This is the end of innocence.
The end of fears, hopes, everlasting "understanding"
and childish dreams that—until now—
lived only inside of me.

The game is over—
And I couldn't care less about anything
anymore.

I am back again!
With my feet firmly standing on this
sacred soil of mine,
Sucking my presence and my past into the

whirlwind of history.

This is the end of me.

I came here to die.

For I have started to live my very own

dream.

mICHAEL'S cONFESSION

It runs deep

Under the skin

In the droplets of clouds

Behind the halo of the moon

Under the rocks of humiliation

In the golden letters of a headstone

In the silent prayer of the earth

In Rebecca's tears

In Alien's eyes

In Victor's generosity

Under the wheels of the skateboard

In runaway dreams

In pain, love, and defiance

Behind the walls of St. Luke's Place

The truth about me

mY cITY

It has a life of its own

Even when I am not there

To protect it and watch over it

It breathes with the millions of wishes

And grows on a myriad of aspirations

both of the blessed and the damned

High into the sky

And then even higher

Until it pierces the very heart of heaven

My City

tHE rEVENGE OF THE dAMNED

In silence of the crisp air
The song of the dead birds
Rises from the wounds of the virgin snow
Cut by the edges of my snowboard

Meekness of the moment
Evaporates like an illusion butchered by the spears
Of the riding Knights of Reality

Letting darkness wrap its arms around the sinful light
Of a streetlamp in front of my window
Barely illuminating a shadow looming over my body
As if suspended in the air by the strings of hesitation
And lust
Before the sudden awareness of the paranormal:
Somehow, this will be its last feast . . .

Anyway

Flesh meets flesh in a high tide of

Revulsion, sorrow, loathing, sadness, and revenge

Sucking in with booze-intoxicated breath of

My mother's husband

My sister's father

My stepfather

My torturer

And undesired lover

If you enjoyed these poems, then check out my novel *Cruel Summer*, the story behind Michael's poetry.

A young skater craving independence. A brutal stepfather bent on controlling him. Is friendship enough to help him when tragedy strikes?

Afterward

On the informational highway, I have traveled for weeks with the headless and destructive speed in an uncommon pursuit of the copyright owner of poetry that captivated me on the first verse. Browsing the websites of the skateboarding equipment manufacturers for other, personal reasons, I ran by chance into the section of so-called skateboarding poetry.

It all started on iskatefakie.com, where under the title *A Tribute to Michael Daniels* I read a few poems of the same author. From there I linked myself to michaeldaniels.com where, without much hesitation, I gave my credit card number to gain access for the symbolic sum of one American dollar to other poems of this young, American poet.

Since I am not a literary critic, and my mother taught me that if I don't have something nice to say about others, I better keep my mouth shut and say nothing, I will let Michael Daniels's poetry speak for itself. However, I cannot say nothing about my sensory perception and experience which a seventeen-year-old, native New Yorker, crazy lover of skateboarding and everything connected with it and a true child of the streets where he won a name for himself, had left me in.

And that sensation was deep and truly experienced. In a cocktail of melancholy, sorrow, hunger, desire, and a love for life, Michael Daniels's poetry is a fine mixture of Rimbaud's, Shakespeare's, and Jim Carroll's poetry. While showing respect to these great, poetic role models, Daniels's poetry remains peculiar, recognizable, and unique.

Daniels's poetry is full of imagery and symbolism; for some readers, it may be too dark or even too brutal. But one should always keep in mind the traumatic experiences in which he created it. (For example, many years of abuse and blackmail by his stepfather, a failed relationship with his girlfriend, the death of his mother.) Having this in mind, Michael's poetry, despite his personal good, cheerful, and generous nature, is raw, cruel, dark, and rough. ("Heart," "The Stealer of Dreams," "Death Can Dance," "Liberation," "Metamorphosis.")

In contrast to this work are his other poems, delicate, gentle, emotional, nostalgic, dreamy, filled with an inexhaustible source of love for his mother, friends, life, and especially for skateboarding ("Summer Symphony," "Unfinished Poem," "A Cacophony of Words," "Departure," "Haiku"); some poems are even titled by the manufacturers of the skateboarding outfit!

Between these two extremes, one can find a few, romantically-themed poems: "A Postcard," "You're Not Here," "Providence," "Spring," "The Bloody River," and a very unusual trilogy in-spired by the "addiction" of young people in America (and beyond) with refreshment drinks, whose producer is doing well enough so I do not feel proper and necessary to mention it here.

How can we characterize and sum up Daniels's poetry in one word? The avant-garde? Extravagant? Alternative? Underground? It is difficult to pinpoint the exact word, as his poetry encompasses all these descriptors. Maybe that is why all attempts at categorizing Michael Daniels in a recognizable framework to facilitate the acceptance, understanding, and identification with it can be found all over the skateboarding websites that contain at least one of Michael's poems as *A Tribute to Michael Daniels*, especially when it comes to Michael Daniels's official website, whose creators are Michael's closest friends, proven exceptional skaters and quality young people—Alien and Victor.

To these two I owe special gratitude (plus something else) for not being too suspicious to respond to my call for help and connect me with Michael's sister, Rebecca Daniels. With almost no financial compensation and already after only a few exchanged e-mails, Rebecca allowed me to present part of her brother's work here. By my choice and led by the internal (and hopefully unmistakable) feeling, with the Daniels sister's blessing, I have chosen about sixty of Michael's poems to present in the collection of selected poems titled *Postcards From Beyond Reality*.

For those who would like to get to know Michael Daniels better than just reading a brief biography on these pages, I invite you to look for the novel *Cruel Summer* and read it. It is the story of Michael Daniels and his friends, told from the perspective of its two actors—Victor and

Alien—and written through the keyboard of the author of
this Afterward.

Bernard Jan

Reviews

Thank you for reading my poetry book *Postcards From Beyond Reality: The Selected Poems of Michael Daniels*. Please consider leaving an honest review on Amazon and Goodreads. Even a sentence or two makes a huge difference, and I will appreciate them. Your honest review generates a beacon of light to other readers seeking books to enjoy. Books that take them elsewhere, into different worlds and other lives, as they get lost between their pages.

Thank you for that.

Please also leave your honest review for my other books if you have read them: *Cruel Summer, January River, Look for Me Under the Rainbow,* and *A World Without Color.*

Acknowledgements

Also, this time, I wasn't alone on my writing journey. First, I want to thank my parents, Ksenija and Dubravko, for their love and continuous support. A huge thanks goes to Vlatko Pavletić who is no longer with us but who was the main "culprit" that these poems saw the light of day in Croatian magazine Forum. Many thanks go to my editors and proofreaders, Editing Sweetheart Claudette Cruz and the Hyper-Speller from wordrefiner.com, my first reader and a good friend, Thomas Carley Jr., and my cover designer, Jessica Bell. Big thanks to Bryan Cohen and Chez Churton, Jen Lassalle, Scarlett Moss, Caz Woolley, Charlene Perry, Quinn Ward, Marcel Liemant, John Phythyon, and everyone else from the Author Ad School Squad and the Best Page Forward team who are amazing in so many ways. I also thank to all my (early) readers and reviewers and everyone who in any way supported this book. Huge thanks go to two special Michaels: Michael Evans, for being such a great indie author and an awesome young man and support, and to my fictional character, Michael Daniels, for being an incredible inspiration for writing my novel *Cruel Summer* and the poetry book *Postcards From Beyond Reality: The Selected Poems of Michael Daniels*. (Please, don't confuse these two Michaels as I often do!) Although you live in my head and heart only, you were my muse for writing these two books and I thank you for that. And, finally, thank you all for reading and liking these poems, and for keeping them and Michael alive.

Share What You Love
(About the Author)

If you liked my writing and enjoyed reading my poetry *Postcards From Beyond Reality: The Selected Poems of Michael Daniels*, please visit my website, where you can find other books I wrote and stay in touch with me by subscribing to my mailing list, reading my blog Muse, or just emailing me.

bernardjanofficial.wixsite.com/bernardjan

I encourage you to check out and read *Cruel Summer, January River, Look for Me Under the Rainbow,* and *A World Without Color.*

Besides being passionate about books, I'm also an animal rights advocate and environmentalist. Helping others and spreading kindness, love, and empathy toward every living creature plays an important role in my life.

If I'm your kind of guy, you are welcome to connect with me and follow me on my favorite social networks via my linktr.ee/bernardjan.

There is no greater joy than to share what you love with those who appreciate it.

Thanks for your time, love, and support!

BJ

Acclaim for Bernard Jan

CRUEL SUMMER

"I was impressed with the insight and empathy of the writer into the spirits of his characters. Any aspiring fiction writer will learn a lot about character development by reading *Cruel Summer* by Bernard Jan. Highly recommended."

—Píaras Ó Cíonnaoíth for Emerald Book Reviews

"I enjoyed the detailed skateboarding stunt instructions at the start of each chapter. His characters were brilliantly written and very compelling."

—Rolanda Lyles for Readers' Favorite

"This singular novel features young adult drama, the trauma of cruel abuse, a time-distorted version of New York City, and some adequately mind-blowing twists . . . Jan's writing style provides an unforgettable, trippy reading experience. The pace moves fast and the plot is completely unexpected . . . *Cruel Summer* is an original and innovative novel that truly knows no bounds."

—Nicky Flowers for Indies Today

Cruel Summer Extract

"MOTHER, I KNOW YOU CAN'T HEAR ME, but I must talk to you.

"I need to talk to someone. Anyone. About things I would never say if you were alive. About things I didn't want you to know because they would hurt you. This way I will say them, and you won't hear them. This way it will be much easier for me to pour my heart out to you . . .

"Mama, I'm not happy. Nothing's been good since you've been gone. I'm lost in a world I do not understand, and I am trying to find myself. I despise so many things, and there is so little worth living for. Worth suffering for. So little.

"You were one of them. You were one of my reasons to keep fighting. As I was one of your reasons you loved to live. I know that, Mother. I know that very well. Although sometimes you used to drive me crazy with your excessive care. With too much attention. You have to understand—I was no longer a child. And you still cared for me.

"Somehow I miss all that now. I need something to keep me going. To guide me. I need someone to give me a reason to try.

"I miss our talks the most. Our plans. There's nothing left. Everything became meaningless. Pointless. Everything is so hard.

"It's cold. It's snowing. But you don't feel it. Time has stopped for you. It's waiting for a better moment.

"I shouldn't be telling you this, but I'm thinking of quitting school. Father would kill me if he knew. That's why I won't tell him. At least not for now. It would kill you to hear me say that. But I have to tell you, Mama. I have to tell someone. I have to confide in someone.

"I see no point in going to school anymore. And I don't feel like going to school, to be honest. I'll dedicate myself to skateboarding and try to make a living out of it for a while. My first contest will be soon, Mama! Lenny already offered to sponsor me. He'll give me as many free shoes and boards as I need. I just have to hang around the city every day and skate, it's my obligation to him. Cool, right? Other skateboarding companies haven't called me yet, but I am expecting their reply any day now. Their sponsorship would mean a lot to me. Not only financially, but also as moral encouragement. It is very important for skaters with the ambition to someday become pro to have someone with a name behind them. Someone who believes in you.

"It means a lot to me, Mama. Skateboarding is my life. Don't be angry about that. I think about my future and that's why I decided to take that step. I think I'm good enough to accomplish something. I think I'm well prepared to win that contest. I could make some money, Mama. Could have already made it, had I not been so hesitant, indecisive, and stupid! Everyone tells me I'm crazy for not competing. I didn't take them seriously; I didn't believe them, and I made a mistake. I must not repeat the same mistake again. At least this time I will give it a try. I have a good feeling I won't disappoint us, Ma. In the end, I'm doing this partly because of you. For you and our shared dream. Which will never become reality because you're gone. But I didn't give up on it. It's just that I must live it myself now.

Please leave your honest review on Amazon.

Table of Contents

www.ingramcontent.com/pod-product-compliance
Lightning Source LLC
Chambersburg PA
CBHW071532150726
48000CB00002B/777